DISASTER PREPAREDNESS

Simple Steps for Businesses

Julie Freestone and Rudi Raab

A FIFTY-MINUTE™ SERIES BOOK

:50™

Viva Books Private Limited
New Delhi • Mumbai • Chennai • Kolkata • Bangalore

First Indian Edition 2004

VIVA BOOKS PRIVATE LIMITED

- 4262/3 Ansari Road, Daryaganj, New Delhi 110 002
  E-mail: viva@vivagroupindia.net
- 215-216 New Apollo Estate, 2nd Floor, Mogra Lane, Andheri (E), Mumbai 400 069
  E-mail: vivamumbai@vivagroupindia.net
- Jamal Fazal Chambers, 26 Greams Road, Chennai 600 006
  E-mail: vivachennai@vivagroupindia.net
- B-103, Jindal Towers, 21/1A/3 Darga Road, Kolkata 700 017
  E-mail: vivakolkata@vivagroupindia.net
- 7 GF, Sovereign Park Apts., 56-58 K.R. Road, Basavanagudi, Bangalore 560 004
  E-mail: vivabangalore@vivagroupindia.net

Published by arrangement with

Crisp Publications, Inc.
1200 Hamilton Court,
Menlo Park
CA 94025
USA

Credits:
Managing Editor: Kathleen Barcos
Production: Barbara Atmore
Typesetting: ExecuStaff
Cover Design: Carol Harris

ISBN 81-7649-552-2

Published by Vinod Vasishtha for Viva Books Private Limited, 4262/3 Ansari Road, Daryaganj, New Delhi 110 002 and printed & bound by Raj Press, R-3 Inderpuri, New Delhi 110 012.

LEARNING OBJECTIVES FOR:

DISASTER PREPAREDNESS

The objectives for *Disaster Preparedness* are listed below. They have been developed to guide you, the reader, to the core issues covered in this book.

Objectives

- ❑ **1) To explain how to set up a disaster plan and why to do it.**

- ❑ **2) To suggest ways that disasters can be prevented.**

- ❑ **3) To discuss how to respond to a disaster.**

- ❑ **4) To summarize recovery and restoration activities.**

Assessing Your Progress

In addition to the Learning Objectives, Crisp, Inc. has developed an **assessment** that covers the fundamental information presented in this book. A twenty-five item, multiple choice/true-false questionnaire allows the reader to evaluate his or her comprehension of the subject matter. An answer sheet with a summary matching the questions to the listed objectives is also available. To learn how to obtain a copy of this assessment please call: **1-800-442-7477** and ask to speak with a Customer Service Representative.

ABOUT THE AUTHORS

Julie Freestone is a member of the Disaster Preparedness Task Force for the Contra Costa County Public Health Division in Martinez, California. For ten years, she was a reporter in the San Francisco Bay Area, covering disaster preparedness and disasters such as the Loma Prieta Earthquake and the East Bay Hills fire, which destroyed more than 1,000 homes.

Rudi Raab is a Berkeley, California, police officer and former police dispatcher who has responded to disasters such as power outages, earthquakes, hazardous materials spills, fires and other calamities. The first disaster he responded to, as a member of the German Red Cross, was in 1962 when a flood caused thousands to be forced from their homes and 300 people died.

ABOUT THE SERIES

With over 200 titles in print, the acclaimed Crisp 50-Minute™ series presents self-paced learning at its easiest and best. These comprehensive self-study books for business or personal use are filled with exercises, activities, assessments, and case studies that capture your interest and increase your understanding.

Other Crisp products, based on the 50-Minute books, are available in a variety of learning style formats for both individual and group study, including audio, video, CD-ROM, and computer-based training.

ACKNOWLEDGMENTS

We've seen, firsthand, some mind-boggling disasters. The Loma Prieta earthquake destroyed portions of the San Francisco Bay Bridge and much more. The Oakland/East Bay Hills fire wiped out an unbelievable 3,354 homes and 456 apartments. We've also seen events such as toxic spills, blizzards, floods, hurricanes, tornadoes, and workplace violence that have brought businesses to a grinding halt and wreaked havoc on personal and professional lives.

We wrote this book to help managers and employees think ahead about what could happen in a disaster and to plan for it before it's too late. Whether you are ready or not, there is every likelihood that some kind of disaster is in your future.

We dedicate this book to the 25 people who lost their life in the East Bay Hills Fire and to others who have died needlessly as a result of disaster around the world.

The authors thank the following for their expert and excellent advice and suggestions:

Edward Galvan, Alameda County (California) Sheriff's Office Search and Rescue Unit

Dan Guerra, Emergency Preparedness Manager, Contra Costa County (California) Health Services Department

Paul Kraintz, Administrator, Contra Costa County Public Health Division

Mike Lash of Lash Glass, Chico, California

Ed Myers of Myers Insurance Agency, San Leandro, California

Jim Valley of Wheelskins, Berkeley, California

CONTENTS

CONTENTS (continued)

PART I

The Importance of Disaster Planning

THE IMPORTANCE OF DISASTER PLANNING

When we think about disasters, what often come to mind first are earthquakes, hurricanes, tornadoes, and other natural disasters that create havoc for businesses and homeowners. We know that natural disasters can happen in every community, anywhere in the world. If we haven't experienced firsthand a natural disaster such as the Northridge quake that damaged 86,000 buildings in Southern California, and Gulf Coast Hurricane Andrew which left 10,000 homeless, then we've read about floods, winter storms, and tornadoes that have destroyed communities and businesses.

But disasters aren't only those that affect whole communities. Fires, water-main breaks, explosions, hazardous material spills, and workplace violence are smaller-scale disasters that can disrupt businesses and result in millions of dollars in damage.

And because we live in a global marketplace, where the world is "shrinking" every year, a disaster in another community miles or even a continent away may affect your business almost as profoundly as a calamity in your own backyard.

Disaster Preparedness Is Good Business

Think of disaster preparedness as good business. Often, in order to survive and prosper, a company must continually develop new products and services and new marketing strategies. Disaster preparedness is a marketing tool.

When a disaster strikes, it may strike you and your competitors simultaneously. If that happens, you and your competition will be racing to restart operations. If you are prepared, your business can be up and running when the others are still trying to explain why they cannot deliver as promised. Should disaster strike only your company while sparing your competitors, it is even more essential that you are prepared to restart operations in a quick, orderly, controlled, and planned fashion.

Expensive advertisement campaigns are designed to take market shares from the competition and to build a loyal customer base. Disaster preparedness can accomplish the same objectives and much more.

WHAT IS A DISASTER?

It depends on your point of view. What a large company can handle as a little annoyance might be, for a small company, a major calamity. Anything that injures or kills people, damages equipment or facilities, or disrupts or shuts down operations can be a disaster.

The good news is that even if you can't prevent all disasters, you can mitigate or reduce the effect they have on your business. And you might discover when you start your disaster planning that some of the steps you take might actually prevent a disaster from happening at all.

Could It Happen to Your Company?

No one wants to spend a lot of time preparing for something that will never happen. To help you decide whether you should go through the disaster planning steps outlined in this book, work through this simple checklist.

Which of these events would be disastrous to your organization?

	YES	NO
A fire damages or destroys the building my business is in.	❑	❑
The inventory, supplies, or equipment used in my business are damaged or destroyed by an explosion, a fire, a flood, an earthquake, or another event.	❑	❑
Records, inventory, supplies, or equipment used in my business are damaged or destroyed by a broken water main.	❑	❑
A power outage lasting at least 24 hours makes it impossible for my company to function or results in problems with our computer system or another equipment.	❑	❑
A heat wave makes it impossible for employees to work and damages or destroys equipment or inventory.	❑	❑

	YES	NO
A strike by a mail service or communications company prevents our receiving orders, shipping orders, or in some other way interrupts customer contact.	❑	❑
A disaster in another city or country involves one or more of our suppliers.	❑	❑
Although my company is spared, a disaster in the community affects more than half of my employees, making it impossible for them to get to work.	❑	❑

Most businesses are probably vulnerable to many of the scenarios in the checklist. Even if you answered yes to only one of these scenarios, your company could benefit from the simple disaster planning described in this book. As you can see, even if the disaster doesn't hit your company or your city directly, you might still need a contingency plan.

WHY PLAN?

> *"Like most people, I assumed little could be done to mitigate the consequences of Nature's wrath. I was stunned to learn just how wrong my own fatalistic thinking about natural disasters was. We need to design our lifestyles, buildings, roads, and bridges to respect Nature's power. And we need to know before disaster happens, not afterwards, how to respond and then cope with recovery and reconstruction."*
>
> —Lawrence Gross, former president of PBS and NBC News[1]

Here are a few revealing statistics that demonstrate the kind of loss your company may experience because of a disaster:

► Experts say that the average company will lose two to three percent of its gross sales within eight days of a sustained computer outage. Fifty percent of companies that experience a power outage lasting more than 10 days will be out of business in five years.[2]

► After the 1989 Loma Prieta earthquake in Northern California, it was estimated that businesses in Santa Cruz suffered $500 million in damage; in Watsonville, $175 million. As many as 5,000 employees were displaced countrywide, and more than 30 businesses had at least $500,000 worth of damage. After a 1983 earthquake in Central California, one-fourth of the businesses in Coalinga closed permanently.[3]

► A fire at a food processing plant killed 25 people, devastating a small town and driving the company out of business.

It seems obvious that doing some kind of disaster planning can help. How?

- Mitigating hazards can save lives, prevent injuries, and help reduce financial losses from damaged or destroyed inventory, equipment, and facilities.

- Identifying the critical functions of your company and figuring out how they could be performed even if operations are disrupted can keep your business operating.

- Disaster planning can help you determine whether you have adequate insurance coverage so that you collect on damaged equipment or for lost business.

- Coping with a disaster effectively can give you an edge over your competition and enhance the image of your company as a reliable and progressive operation.

- The disaster planning effort can be a valuable team-building experience that reaps benefits for the company's operations and morale overall.

- Showing employees that the company is prepared for a disaster can create a sense of security and loyalty.

PART II

Setting Up Your Company's Plan

WHAT IS DISASTER PLANNING?

Organizations such as the American Red Cross and the Federal Emergency Management Agency (FEMA) specialize in assisting organizations with extensive, comprehensive disaster or emergency planning, called *business resumption planning*. This book is not intended to replace those ongoing, dynamic efforts that are a part of the company's operations in the same way that human resources and finance departments are. But not every company is able to or ready to undertake comprehensive disaster planning efforts, and that's where this book comes in. It helps to think about disaster planning in three steps: before, during and after.

STEP #1: Before

Prevention/Mitigation: This is the step in which business owners assess and correct or reduce any hazards that might cause injuries or damage during a disaster. In this step, the business anticipates what might occur, puts into place systems and supplies that enable responding to a disaster, and encourages employees and suppliers to do likewise.

STEP #2: During

Response: Using a predetermined plan, employees and principals in the business perform functions immediately following a disaster to protect lives and ensure the continuation of operations following the disaster. Training and drills make it possible for everyone to perform as needed.

STEP #3: After

Recovery and Restoration: In this step, using a predetermined plan, the company is able to maintain essential functions, having identified such things as alternate locations, alternate suppliers/vendors, methods of maintaining client/customer contact, and data collection for insurance and/or disaster relief purposes. Repairs are made, new equipment is acquired, business loans are arranged, and full functioning is restored.

> “*Effective business resumption planning requires senior management commitment measured in dollars and resources. This commitment must be sustained, even after an effective plan has been put together. . . . Plans must be living and dynamic. Selling the benefits of long term planning to an organization that has daily crises and production needs is an art!*”
>
> —California Office of Emergency Services[4]

WHO SHOULD BE IN CHARGE?

In every company, there must be an individual or a group who is in charge of developing the disaster plan and keeping it updated. This person/group must ensure that everyone in the company knows about the plan and his or her role in implementing it, should a disaster strike.

Who should that person or group be? In a small company, it could be the owner or chief executive officer. It could be a secretary, volunteer, or any employee who is organized, committed to the development of the plan, and likely to remain with the company for a substantial period of time. In a larger company, the planning committee can include representatives of the various organization functions.

Regardless of whether it is one person or a formal committee, it is important that

- Senior management is committed to developing the plan.
- Every department/function in the company knows the plan is being developed and has a chance to provide input into its elements.
- The committee or individual developing and coordinating the plan has access to the resources needed to implement the plan.
- There is a clear statement describing the purpose of the effort.

TAKING ACTION

Tools for Taking Action

As you work your way through this book, you'll find sections called **Taking Action.** These sections contain memos, checklists and other tools you can use to actually begin your planning efforts and keep them on track.

TAKING ACTION

In many cases, you'll be asked to identify dates when specific tasks will be done. Use the planner below to write down tasks to be done and their planned completion dates. You may want to transfer these dates to an office calendar.

Six-Month Planner

Month of ____________	**Month of** ____________
Task #1 ____________	**Task #1** ____________
Date to be completed ____________	**Date to be completed** ____________
Task #2 ____________	**Task #2** ____________
Date to be completed ____________	**Date to be completed** ____________
Task #3 ____________	**Task #3** ____________
Date to be completed ____________	**Date to be completed** ____________
Task #4 ____________	**Task #4** ____________
Date to be completed ____________	**Date to be completed** ____________
Month of ____________	**Month of** ____________
Task #1 ____________	**Task #1** ____________
Date to be completed ____________	**Date to be completed** ____________
Task #2 ____________	**Task #2** ____________
Date to be completed ____________	**Date to be completed** ____________
Task #3 ____________	**Task #3** ____________
Date to be completed ____________	**Date to be completed** ____________
Task #4 ____________	**Task #4** ____________
Date to be completed ____________	**Date to be completed** ____________
Month of ____________	**Month of** ____________
Task #1 ____________	**Task #1** ____________
Date to be completed ____________	**Date to be completed** ____________
Task #2 ____________	**Task #2** ____________
Date to be completed ____________	**Date to be completed** ____________
Task #3 ____________	**Task #3** ____________
Date to be completed ____________	**Date to be completed** ____________
Task #4 ____________	**Task #4** ____________
Date to be completed ____________	**Date to be completed** ____________

LEARNING FROM EXPERIENCE

We can learn something from the experiences of other companies that have faced disasters and survived. Here's what happened to California Federal Savings and Loan at their four-story main headquarters during a 1987 earthquake in Southern California:

> The earthquake hit at 7:42 A.M. with only 75 people in the building. [Had it been] an hour later, 1,000 employees would have been there. Power and telephone service went out immediately; exterior windows broke and fell outward as designed but interior glass walls shattered. Emergency generators broke free of their mountings, but they were automatically shut down when leaks from broken water pipes caused extensive damage. The emergency lighting system failed. Dust from the partial collapse of a suspended ceiling in the computer room was misinterpreted (by automatic sensing devices) as smoke and triggered the dumping of Halon, a chemical that sucks all oxygen out of the air.
>
> Fortunately the computer room was not fully staffed at the time. Over 90,000 ceiling tiles were dislodged, replaced, and dislodged [again] during a subsequent aftershock. Personnel had to crawl over upended furniture in complete darkness to evacuate the building. Because the in-house centralized phone system was destroyed, a command center was established in the parking lot, using a car phone. The cellular phone company cut off service to the car phone several hours later for overusage. In order to send crews to the company's alternate data processing site in Phoenix, bank officials had to break into their own nonfunctioning ATM machines to provide cash for the trip.[5]

A STATEMENT OF OBJECTIVE

Write a statement that explains to the individual/committee, and to the entire organization, the purpose of the disaster planning effort. Keep it simple. Here is a sample:

SAMPLE STATEMENT

Disaster Planning Objective

The Disaster Planning Effort of the XYZ Company is established to create a plan in the event of a disaster. The plan will describe how company employees will respond to preserve lives, minimize injuries, and ensure the least disruption of the company operations and the most effective restoration of operations.

Now see how you can adapt this sample for your own situation.

YOUR COMPANY'S STATEMENT

Disaster Planning Objective

MAKING THE ANNOUNCEMENT

Once your objective is completed, there are a few other simple issues to be resolved. Announcing the planning effort to employees is an important step because it underscores the importance of the planning and demonstrates top management's concern and commitment. Consider these issues:

- Who will be designated to oversee the planning process?
- When will the announcement be made?
- What is your timeframe for completion?
- How will the organization be informed of the commitment?
- What process will the individual or committee use to acquire resources needed in planning?

Here is a sample announcement. Make changes in it to reflect your writing style and your company's need.

Sample Announcement Letter

To: All Box Paper Employees

From: Jack Ream, President

Subject: Disaster Planning

I am pleased to announce the appointment of Mary Smith as our new Disaster Preparedness Coordinator. She will be overseeing the development of a comprehensive disaster plan that will involve every employee and department.

I have directed her to establish a committee that will create a plan to be used in the event of a disaster. The plan will describe how all of us will respond to save lives and reduce injuries, making it possible for us to survive immediately following a disaster and ensure the least disruption and the most effective restoration of operations.

An important part of Mary's role will be coordinating the preparation of All Box's disaster plan. She will also be encouraging each of you to develop personal disaster plans that will help you and your families.

We hope to have a drafted plan completed within six months. Please give Mary your full cooperation as she launches this most important activity.

Now write your own announcement. With these steps done, you are on the road to helping your company be prepared!

GETTING READY

Before you can begin planning, you have to consider what kinds of disaster might strike, what problems might be caused, and what impact the problems would have on your company, employees, and customers.

In the upcoming Taking Action you'll find a chart that you can use to establish some of the assumptions that will provide the foundation for your disaster planning. Enter in columns A, B, and C the names of three disasters you think are most likely to happen in your community. Here are some possibilities.

- *Natural Disasters:* Heat- or coldwave, flood, fire, drought, earthquake, ice storm or blizzard, tornado.
- *Other Disasters:* Broken water main, plane crash, workplace violence/ bombing, hazardous material, spill, explosion.

For each of these events, enter a number indicating how likely it is that the disaster you described would cause the problem listed. Entering 5 indicates a high probability; 0 indicates the lowest probability. The lower the total score, the lower your company's vulnerability. Here is an example:

PREDICTING DISASTER-RELATED PROBLEMS			
Resulting Problems	**A. Disaster:** Flood	**B. Disaster:** Fire	**C. Disaster:** Blizzard
Power outage	5	5	3
Communications failure	3	5	3
Roads closed	4	2	5
Mail stopped	3	2	5
Employees out	4	1	5
Building locked down	4	5	1
Data banks out	2	2	2
Inventory damaged	4	5	1
Water outage	4	4	1
TOTALS	33	31	26

Probability: Enter a number from 0 (No way) to 5 (Highly likely)

TAKING ACTION

On the form that follows, enter in columns A, B, and C the three disasters most likely to happen at your workplace. For each event, write the number representing the likelihood such a disaster would cause the problem listed, 0 being least likely and 5 being highly likely.

PREDICTING DISASTER-RELATED PROBLEMS

Resulting Problems	A. Disaster: ________	B. Disaster: ________	C. Disaster: ________
Power outage			
Communications failure			
Roads closed			
Mail stopped			
Employees out			
Building locked down			
Data banks out			
Inventory damaged			
Water outage			
Other:			
TOTALS			

Among those problems identified as having a high probability (a score of 3 or higher) circle the ones that would have a significant impact on your business. Would it have a significant impact if it lasted for more than 24 hours? More than three days? More than a week?

We'll reexamine these problems later, in Steps 2 and 3 when we talk more about disaster response and recovery planning. Give yourself and your company a pat on the back for taking an honest look at what disasters might happen and their possible impact on your operations.

PART III

Step One: Prevention and Mitigation

TAKING STOCK OF HAZARDS

Although it is not possible to prevent most disasters, you *can* prevent some of them. In many cases, with a bit of prevention, you can reduce the injuries and damage that result from the disaster.

In general, workplace hazards that can be mitigated to prevent injury and damage during a disaster fall into two categories: structural and nonstructural.

Structural Hazards

These are the dangers that may exist in your actual office/plant structure.

- In earthquake country, hazards include buildings that are made of unreinforced masonry; structures that are not bolted to their foundations; and inner walls constructed in a manner that allows the upper floors of the building to collapse or "pancake" on lower floors.

- In areas where flooding is likely, structural hazards could be windows or doors that allow water to enter the structure.

- If one or more of your buildings is constructed near or on the border of wildland areas, hazards include fire danger from accumulated dead leaves and debris; flammable vegetation; overhanging branches; and unsafe roofing materials such as cedar shakes.

- Non-fire-resistant building materials and inadequate sprinkler systems also constitute hazards.

- Structural hazards might also include inadequate exits that hamper evacuation of employees and removal of equipment.

- In the area around the facility, rivers, dams, or other bodies of water, or faulty drainage constitute flood danger. Toxic materials, as well, constitute potential hazards.

TAKING STOCK OF HAZARDS (continued)

To eliminate hazards in leased facilities, work with the building owner to reduce danger. Begin by identifying hazards. Review the terms and conditions of your lease to determine who is responsible for mitigating problems. Be sure to determine whether there are provisions in your lease for suspending rent payments if the building is too damaged to be usable after a disaster.

Use this worksheet to identify hazards and take actions to correct them.

STRUCTURAL HAZARDS WORKSHEET					
Hazard Identified	Action/ Solution	Person Responsible	Date Due	Cost	Date Completed

Nonstructural Hazards

Even more prevalent are nonstructural hazards—those objects in the office or plant that could fall, move, or break and cause injury or damage. Luckily, these hazards are easier to correct.

The rule of thumb is to ensure that these elements are secured in a manner that will prevent injury to employees and customers and will protect inventory and equipment from damage in the event of building movement.

Here is a list of some of the nonstructural hazards you might encounter. There may be other nonstructural hazards that you want to add to it. Use the checklist that follows to walk around your facility and identify what needs to be corrected, or have a supervisor in each area complete the checklist in his or her own site. Look for the following items:

- Overhead light fixtures that are not securely attached and could be dislodged in an earthquake, tornado, explosion or other building movement.
- File cabinets, shelves, data cribs, equipment bins, partitions and other office furniture that could topple or roll.
- File cabinet drawers that are not secured and could be dislodged during building movement.
- Fire extinguishers that are not securely hung or are placed in locations where they cannot be seen or are inaccessible to employees, including physically challenged employees.
- Hazardous materials that are improperly stored, are subject to movement or spillage, and/or not labeled for quick identification in the event of a problem.
- Generators and other emergency equipment that are located in an area that is subject to flooding, broken glass, and other hazards.
- Fuel/batteries for emergency equipment that are stored in a manner that would endanger their effective use when needed.
- Heavy objects that are positioned on high shelves and could fall on employees during an earthquake or other movement of the building.

NONSTRUCTURAL HAZARDS WORKSHEET			
Safety Requirements	**Location of Hazard**	**Action Needed**	**Status**
Overhead light fixtures are properly attached.			
File cabinets, shelves, data cribs, equipment bins and other office furniture are secured.			
File cabinet drawers are secured.			
Fire extinguishers are hung properly and are visible and accessible.			
Hazardous materials are properly stored, secured, and labeled.			
Emergency equipment is located in a safe area.			
Emergency fuel/ batteries are stored appropriately.			
No heavy objects are on high shelves.			

LEARNING FROM EXPERIENCE

Many companies have paid the price for not addressing nonstructural hazards before a disaster. After the 1989 Loma Prieta earthquake in Northern California, large corporations such as Pacific Gas and Electric and Pacific Bell reported $45 to $50 million in property damage.[6]

Now that you have identified the structural and nonstructural hazards for your company and taken steps to correct them, you've accomplished one of the most important tasks in protecting the lives of employees and the assets that will be needed to keep the company operating.

TAKING STOCK OF CONTENTS

> When Marijo Whitcomb locked the door to her downtown business (in Grand Forks, North Dakota) as the river threatened, she knew when she returned, nothing would be the same. She was right. Deitz Business Promotion was under water nearly two weeks. Three computer systems, more than 3,000 embroidery discs, a $7,000 solid oak custom-made counter, and all their records were lost. Whitcomb and her husband, Kyle, had no insurance. These days, the business operates from a cubicle in a building on the University of North Dakota campus. Like others here, the Whitcombs are in a holding pattern—waiting for money, contractors, and a new office.[7]

Now that you've examined how to reduce the damage or injury that might result if your company's building is involved in a disaster, take a look at the contents of your business and see what other ways you can prevent damage. Consider your business's records, artwork, inventory, and insurance, as follows:

- **RECORDS:** If you use a computer for recordkeeping, payroll, and other functions, do you have computer files adequately backed up? Is the backup stored off the premises? Can you access it easily after a disaster? How often do you update the backup? Where are the records you need for tax and insurance purposes? Do you have duplicates you can use in case of an emergency? Have you considered what kind of backup material you will need if there is no power to operate your computer system?

- **ARTWORK:** If you have artwork for company stationery, logos, advertising, etc., are there extra copies of the artwork stored off premises in an accessible location? Is the artwork current?

► **INVENTORY:** Is there inventory that is critical to your operations, which might be damaged in disaster? Do you have it stored in the best possible manner? Do you have a way in which you can replace at least part of the inventory quickly following a disaster? Do you have alternate suppliers who wouldn't be affected by the disaster and who know your company?

► **INSURANCE:** After a disaster, one of the most important considerations is insurance. Part of the disaster-planning operation is to include an assessment of your insurance coverage. See page 44 for more information about what areas should be considered. Be sure to store copies of your insurance records in a safe deposit box or other location that will be accessible after a disaster if your main facility is closed.

PART IV

Step Two: Responding

FIRST AID AND RESCUE

When disaster strikes, it is too late to begin deciding what the most critical tasks are and who should do them. This section and its detailed checklists will help you decide beforehand what must be done during and immediately following a disaster; who should perform these tasks; and what training and resources are required to ensure that they are done properly.

> ### *LEARNING FROM EXPERIENCE*
>
> After a disaster in his city, Larry Meredith of the San Francisco Department of Public Health reported that a hot-water pipe broke in the ceiling of the fourth floor of his office building. He said it ran for 10 hours before someone could find the shut-off.[8]

Before considering any impact on the business, it is of course critical that every effort be made to protect the lives of employees and customers and prevent injury and death. To accomplish this, you'll need to address four issues: an evacuation plan, emergency shutdown, CPR-first-aid training, and emergency supplies.

An Evacuation Plan

Every discrete location in your office or plant should have a posted evacuation route. Employees should know the evacuation routes and practice using them. Consider what will be done during an evacuation for individuals, including customers, with special needs.

Emergency Shutdown

As you are planning for evacuation, or while you are assessing the potential damage to the building, determine which building functions might have to be turned off, including water, electricity, and gas. Designate one or more employees to know the location of the shut-off valves and when to shut things off. Find out when it is appropriate—and when it isn't—to turn off the gas. Contact your local utilities for information and assistance.

FIRST AID AND RESCUE (continued)

CPR/First-Aid Training

At least one employee in every work location/floor should be able to administer basic first aid and CPR. Be sure to have someone trained on every shift in each location. Contact the American Red Cross in your community for information about low-cost training. Every facility should be equipped with a first-aid kit and related supplies (see page 37). Use the worksheet on page 35 to keep track of these supplies and employees' certification.

Ensuring that there are employees in your company who are certified in CPR and basic first aid will help in times of disaster and for other emergencies. Recognize the employees who participated in this important step.

FIRST-AID WORKSHEET				
Location/ Floor	First-Aid Kit Location	Nearest Employee Trained in CPR/First Aid	Certification Date of Employee Training	Renewal Dates of Certification

FIRST AID AND RESCUE (continued)

Emergency Supplies

In each location, arrange for appropriate supplies to be on hand to aid in evacuation efforts. It may be necessary, as well, to provide supplies for employees to shelter in place while roads in the area are made passable or until the building is reached by police and fire crews.

Following is a list of suggested supplies that should be in place. In general, supplies should be chosen to be consistent with the type of disaster likely to occur, as predicted in Part I.

In a protracted emergency when employees will have to shelter in place, water supplies are especially important. When stocking emergency water, consider whether your existing water (bottled, in water heaters, and in ice cubes) could be used. Water can be purified by boiling for one to three minutes, or with purification tablets or by adding two to four drops of household bleach to each quart of water.

Companies with cafeterias may not need to store emergency food, but businesses that only have electrically powered vending machines should consider alternate food distribution methods.

LEARNING FROM EXPERIENCE

It's unwise to wait until a disaster strikes to procure supplies. After the 1989 Loma Prieta earthquake, most stores in the San Francisco Bay Area were out of batteries within hours of the disaster.[9]

You are making excellent progress. By working to this point, you've made it possible for employees to be taken care of immediately following a disaster, and to have staff trained in first aid available to assist.

Emergency Supplies

Assigned to: Due Date:

FIRST AID

- ❑ Adhesive tape and bandages
- ❑ Nonaspirin pain reliever (acetaminophen)
- ❑ Waterless and liquid soap
- ❑ Compresses, sanitary pads, and gauze pads
- ❑ Scissors and tweezers
- ❑ Rubber gloves
- ❑ Eye protection

EVACUATION

- ❑ Fire extinguishers and hoses
- ❑ Flashlights (with batteries) and/or lightsticks
- ❑ Soft-bristle paintbrush for glass
- ❑ Tarps
- ❑ Axe, crowbar, saw
- ❑ Propane lantern with fuel
- ❑ Hammers, screwdriver, wrenches, wire cutters
- ❑ Hard hats
- ❑ Masking tape/duct tape
- ❑ Rope
- ❑ Heavyweight gloves
- ❑ Sturdy shoes (work boot-type)

SHELTERING IN PLACE

- ❑ Plastic bags for human excrement
- ❑ Matches
- ❑ One or more space blankets
- ❑ Water (five gallons per day, per person, with one quart for drinking)
- ❑ Can opener
- ❑ Toilet paper
- ❑ Food (e.g., canned meat or fish, dried fruit, peanut butter, granola or energy bars)

ASSIGNING ROLES

During a disaster, individuals may be called upon to perform functions for which they have special training or prior experience. In this section, you will learn how to identify critical functions of your business operations and designate people to oversee the functions following a disaster. The following skills inventory, completed for the employees in your organization, will help you decide upon the most appropriate individuals to designate.

EMPLOYEE SKILLS INVENTORY						
Name/Work Location/ Shift	CPR	First Aid	Computer	Fire Fighters	Language	Other

You've created a very important building block for your disaster response plan. Now you know exactly what skills and resources are available to be assigned following a disaster.

IDENTIFYING CRITICAL COMPANY FUNCTIONS

In addition to ensuring employees' safety, caring for their injuries, and providing necessary food and water, the disaster plan must include a component for minimizing the disaster event's disruption of business operations. To begin that process, identify the critical functions of your organization that will have to be restored in order to carry on minimal functions, and to restore full functioning as soon as practical.

This next chart is designed to help the company's disaster response coordinator determine

- What critical functions will have to be addressed
- Who should be designated to address them
- Where the function will be carried out if the normal location for that function is compromised
- How the function will be conducted and what resources will be required
- How quickly and how often after the disaster the function will have to be performed

Note: It's likely that the most effective way to complete this function identification task is for the disaster response coordinator to enlist the assistance of individuals or departments responsible for the day-to-day operations of each function.

Using the completed employee skills inventory and other personnel information you may have available, tentatively designate who will be responsible for each of the critical functions of your organization. Each designated individual should then complete a detailed plan using the worksheets provided in the Detailed Plans section coming up (pp. 43 through 58). The individuals designated to oversee the critical functions are the members of your Disaster Response Team.

IDENTIFYING CRITICAL COMPANY FUNCTIONS (continued)

ASSIGNMENTS FOR CRITICAL COMPANY FUNCTIONS			
Function	**Who Is Responsible**	**Where/How**	**Completion/ Frequency**
Payroll			
Customer service			
Manufacturing			
Inventory			
Supplies			
Order fulfillment			
Records			
Data/MIS			
Finance			
Insurance			
Human resources			
Facilities			
PR			
Emergency functions			
First aid			
Housing			
Transport rescue			
Evacuation			
Assessment			
Security			

Now you're not working alone. You've created a whole team that will share the responsibility for gathering information and putting your disaster response plan together.

TIPS FOR GETTING THE JOB DONE

This information-gathering phase of your planning effort may seem overwhelming. And it is, in fact, complex and time consuming. Here are a few tips for staying in control and getting the job done:

✔ The disaster preparedness effort can be a valuable team-building experience. To find out about how to work efficiently in teams and produce quick results, consult *Working in Teams: A Team Member Guidebook,* another Crisp Publications 50-Minute book.

✔ Break the information-gathering task down into small components. Set goals. For instance, get one of the checklists completed per week. Or have the person designated to oversee each detailed checklist answer one question per week.

✔ Establish milestones, so you know you're making progress. Some important milestones include assigning the disaster response teams; designating a location for the Emergency Communications Center (discussed in Step Three); getting out your first newsletter; completing the employee skills inventory.

✔ Reward yourself and your Disaster Response Team when you've achieved milestones. Have a pizza party; give out batteries or transistor radios or other disaster supplies.

✔ Recognize people who are giving their time and attention to getting the planning done. Mention their names in your newsletter; write a commendation to their supervisors; frame a certificate of achievement (see sample in next Taking Action section).

✔ Delegate responsibility for getting answers and information. Besides making your job easier, this sharing of responsibility encourages everyone in the company to take ownership for the plan.

✔ Use outside resources. For example, the American Red Cross and FEMA have excellent pamphlets available on disaster preparedness, containing checklists and guides. Order them and distribute them to employees.

✔ "Push the edge of the envelope" when thinking of ways to address disaster-related issues. Step away from the usual way of doing things and be creative. (The Crisp book, *Creativity in Business* might help!)

TAKING ACTION

Recognizing employees who contribute to disaster planning is an effective way for a company to underscore its commitment to the process. One simple and inexpensive way is to give certificates to those who make outstanding contributions. Here's a sample:

Certificate of Achievement

for

Doris Jones

For her commitment in helping the Box Paper Company prepare for surviving a disaster.

DETAILED PLANS

In the previous section, you identified individuals to oversee each critical function. If your company is large enough, it may be advisable to also establish Task Groups for each area. Members of a Task Group will assist in developing the detailed plan and would implement the plan during a disaster and following it.

As each function overseer and/or Task Group member submits his or her contribution to the detailed plans, log them in on the Assignment Sheet so you can keep track of your progress.

We have provided a list of questions for each of the functions listed in the Assignment worksheet. Answers to these questions will be the basis for your written plan. In addition to using these questions, staff involved in each function should be invited and challenged to identify additional issues and problems that could be addressed.

These questions are intended to provoke thoughts and ideas for a written plan, not as an exhaustive list.

LEARNING FROM EXPERIENCE

According to FEMA, most companies discover that they are not properly insured only after they have suffered a loss. FEMA says lack of appropriate insurance can be financially devastating.[10]

> From [the appearance of] its stately red brick facade, St. Michael's Church (in Grand Forks, North Dakota), seems to have withstood the flood without a scar. Inside, the Rev. William Sherman knows better. Water engulfed the basement of the church and school, wiping out classrooms, offices, day care and a huge communal kitchen—$150,000 in appliances alone were destroyed. Insurance will cover about 20 percent of the $1.4 million in losses. The rest will have to be raised . . . Some of Rev. Sherman's 5,000 parishioners lost houses, some lost jobs and some lost both.

INSURANCE DISCUSSION SHEET

When will you call your insurance agent? ______________________

Where are extra copies of your insurance policies stored? __________

What to Discuss

- ✔ What type of disasters does your insurance cover? What types are *not* covered? Will your policy cover lost income resulting from power outages and other disruptions? Look in the probability chart completed in Part I—are the likely events covered?

- ✔ What can you do in advance to collect the documentation your insurance company needs to reimburse you for losses following a disaster? Should you photograph or videotape your equipment and inventory, for example? Where will you store the documentation so that it is safe and accessible following a disaster? When you are planning your response and recovery system, ensure that it reflects the requirements of your insurance company.

- ✔ Will you be insured for such things as extra costs required to expedite delivery of supplies for manufacturing or customer orders; payments for overtime; employee personal property; cleaning and repair of equipment; costs of temporary help and temporary space?

- ✔ How long will it be before the insurance company issues your reimbursement?

- ✔ Who will you contact immediately following a disaster? What if your local agent is affected by the same disaster?

- ✔ Does your insurance carrier have special discounts for companies actively engaged in disaster preparedness? Are there certain mitigation efforts you should launch to qualify you for the discounts?

- ✔ Does your insurance carrier have disaster preparedness materials that could help you in developing your plan?

You've made a major contribution! By looking at the insurance issues head-on and getting answers to these important questions, you've taken a giant step toward "insuring" the health of the company following a disaster!

PAYROLL WORKSHEET

Assigned to: ______________________ Date Due: ______________

Employees who are already on your payroll will have to be paid, and records will have to be maintained. How will you accomplish that?

- ✔ How will your organization issue checks if there is a disaster?
- ✔ According to the disaster predictions in Part I, how likely is it that the payroll function will be compromised?
- ✔ Is there an outside vendor that you can contact now to establish emergency payroll procedures?
- ✔ How will you pay your employees if the local banks are without power and paychecks cannot be turned into cash?
- ✔ Does your bank have provisions for issuing your company's paychecks during a community-wide disaster?
- ✔ If your computer system is down, how will you maintain payroll records?
- ✔ For employees who work overtime related to the disaster, what special record-keeping provisions will be required?

Comments: ____

____

____

____

____

____

CUSTOMER SERVICE WORKSHEET

Assigned to: ____________________ Date Due: ______________

You've worked hard to build up your customer base. How will you protect it during and following a disaster, when you may not be able to meet customers' needs or even communicate with them? Consider the following:

- ✔ How will you keep in touch with your customers immediately following a disaster and during the recovery period?
- ✔ Would establishing a Web site now be helpful later? Is there someone who could be designated to maintain and service the site during the recovery stage?
- ✔ Is there a phone company service available that would make it possible for your customers to send and receive voice messages to the company while your site is not functioning?

Comments: ____

LEARNING FROM EXPERIENCE

Although California Federal Savings and Loan credits its Business Resumption Plan, completed in June 1987, with saving them from confusion, chaos, and a loss of control following the Northridge earthquake, the business recommends testing all parts of the plan to ensure it works for every department. Customer service had not been included in their plan, and this caused havoc because the company gets an average of 40,000 calls per day from customers.[12]

MANUFACTURING WORKSHEET

Assigned to: ______________________ Date Due: ______________

How will you continue to produce your company's products or services?

✔ Can you set up an off-site skeleton operation?

✔ Do you have sufficient supplies on hand to operate for a period during recovery?

✔ Do you have staff trained to step in as back-up if regular staff are unavailable as a result of the disaster?

✔ Could you subcontract all or part of your manufacturing process to an outside vendor during the recovery period in order to maintain your customer base?

Comments: ____

____

____

____

____

____

INVENTORY WORKSHEET

Assigned to: ______________________ Date Due: ______________

If you have inventory, it no doubt represents both a significant investment as well as a critical element of your operations. How will you protect your inventory and ensure its availability during recovery?

- ✔ Is the company inventory stored to withstand the impact of a disaster as much as possible?
- ✔ How long following a disaster will the inventory remain sufficient for production?
- ✔ Are there alternate methods for replenishing the inventory during the recovery stage?

Comments: ____

____

____

____

____

____

SUPPLIES WORKSHEET

Assigned to: ______________________ Date Due: ______________

To maintain operations, certain supplies must be available even if the vendors and transportation systems normally used are unavailable. How will you ensure that supplies are on hand? Replenished?

✔ Have alternate vendors been identified and contacted? Are these vendors likely to be spared by a local disaster? Are they familiar with your organization's needs?

✔ How will supplies be delivered to your sites if roads are impassible?

✔ Will it be necessary to set up your manufacturing facilities closer to the supplies in order to avoid long-term disruption?

Comments: ____

____

____

____

____

____

LEARNING FROM EXPERIENCE

A disastrous fire in Canada in 1989 destroyed the only plant in North America that supplies the key chemical to fill air bags for automobiles. Major automobile manufacturers could not ship hundreds of thousands of automobiles without the required air bags. TRW, the principal supplier of the air bags, however, had engaged in disaster planning and was able to buy the critical material elsewhere.[13]

"Our philosophy rests on the premise that all businesses can and should have emergency plans . . . If you cannot take care of yourselves, you cannot take care of your customers."—Fil Bernal, Southern California Gas.[14]

ORDER FULFILLMENT WORKSHEET

Assigned to: ______________________ Date Due: ______________

How will customer ordering demand be met during and following a disaster in a manner that will protect your customer base?

- ✔ If mail service, phone service, or transportation and roads are compromised, how will orders be filled?
- ✔ How will customers be notified of delays?
- ✔ Are there other suppliers who would participate with your company in mutual aid arrangements to service client needs during recovery?
- ✔ Do your contracts include nonperformance penalties and are disasters excluded as nonperformance subject to those penalties?

Comments: ____

____

____

____

____

____

Note: Participation in industrial mutual-aid associations is widespread and of proven value, according to the Manufacturers Alliance for Productivity and Innovation (MAPI).[15]

RECORDS WORKSHEET

Assigned to: ______________________ Date Due: ______________

How will you protect your existing records? How will you safeguard records created during a disaster so that you can document operations for disaster-relief purposes?

- ✔ Where will existing records be stored so they can be easily retrieved for insurance reports and loan applications?
- ✔ How will you document expenses during recovery?
- ✔ Will the record system need insurance-carrier and disaster-relief requirements?
- ✔ What should be done now to protect the records in the event of a disaster?

Comments: ____

FINANCE WORKSHEET

Assigned to: ____________________ Date Due: ______________

The flow of cash into and out of the company must continue following a disaster. How will that be accomplished in an effective and efficient manner?

✔ How will Accounts Receivable be handled if mail is disrupted or if your bank is not functioning?

✔ What will be done about Accounts Payable if the usual staff is not available or records are inaccessible?

✔ How will your creditors be notified?

✔ Have you talked with the company's major suppliers about extending credit in the event of a disaster?

✔ What formula will be used to calculate losses for insurance purposes?

Comments: ____

DATA/MIS WORKSHEET

Assigned to: ______________________ Date Due: ______________

Can your existing computer system handle a major disruption?

✔ Is the back-up system adequate and up-to-date?

✔ What hardware will be used if equipment is destroyed?

✔ Is there an outside vendor that can temporarily operate your computer system?

✔ What manual systems can be used during the recovery stage to provide a foundation for eventually recovering lost electronic information?

✔ Have you arranged hardcopy and off-site storage of critical information that will be needed during an emergency?

✔ Are there steps that can be taken now to mitigate the disaster-related damage to computer equipment and records?

Comments: ____

____

____

____

____

____

INSURANCE WORKSHEET

Assigned to: ______________________ Date Due: ______________

To insure that full and proper coverage is achieved for losses suffered during a disaster, it is important to designate responsibility for coordinating insurance issues. Be sure to use the information generated during the prevention stage (Step One).

- ✔ After a disaster occurs, who will be responsible for overseeing the collection of insurance documentation, contacting the insurance carrier, and overseeing timely reimbursement?
- ✔ What record-keeping systems must be created now to provide for adequate documentation?
- ✔ How will employees know about the record-keeping requirements?
- ✔ Arrange an on-site visit by your insurance company's loss control officer.

Comments: ____

____

____

____

____

____

____

LEARNING FROM EXPERIENCE

Bank of America in California reported that in the days following the Loma Prieta earthquake, it offered a variety of aid to employees, including emergency cash grants, time off, flex-time, car pools, and post-traumatic stress counseling.[16]

HUMAN RESOURCES WORKSHEET

Assigned to: ______________________ Date Due: ______________

Maintaining and supporting the workforce during and following a disaster is a critical element in achieving full recovery.

- ✔ How will employees be paid if the company's regular payroll system is compromised?
- ✔ Is there an outside vendor who can be contacted now to arrange assistance in processing your payroll?
- ✔ What timesheets and other personnel records must be maintained during the recovery stage for insurance and other purposes?
- ✔ Do you need to expand or amend HR policies to provide for employees who are unable to arrive at work for a prolonged period of time because of a disaster?
- ✔ What is the company policy regarding calling in employees if the disaster occurs during off-hours?
- ✔ Will the company allow flexible hours and modified work weeks?
- ✔ What is the policy regarding the use of leave to handle family emergencies during the disaster?
- ✔ How will the company handle lay-offs of employees whose jobs are nonessential during recovery?
- ✔ What are the company's expectations about overtime and what will be the policy for overtime pay?
- ✔ What temporary employees might be needed during the recovery stage? Who is responsible for hiring them? Could a temp agency be briefed now about the company's needs?

Comments: ____

____

____

FACILITIES WORKSHEET

Assigned to: ______________________ Date Due: ______________

During a disaster, the facilities of a company are often the most obviously damaged, and repairing the problems quickly and efficiently is vital to the recovery.

- ✔ Are phone numbers posted in a prominent place that can be read from the outside of the facility, indicating who should be contacted in case of an after-hours emergency?
- ✔ If you are leasing your building(s), what does your lease say about the party responsible for repairs after a disaster? Do you know whom to call to make the arrangements for repairs? Who is responsible for communicating with the building owner to make necessary repairs?
- ✔ Who is responsible for assessing the building and other facilities to determine the extent of the damage following the disaster?
- ✔ What contractors are available locally to assist in clean-up and repair?
- ✔ Are there emergency generators in your building? Do you need one or more alternate sources of power? Do you or someone on staff know how to connect it? Have you decided which equipment will be powered by the generator?
- ✔ What can local utilities do to help?
- ✔ How will the decision be made to evacuate? To shelter in place? To turn off utilities?
- ✔ Are propane tanks, air compressors, and other equipment bolted down?

Comments: ____

____

____

____

____

LEARNING FROM EXPERIENCE

An Alumax plant in South Carolina learned firsthand during Hurricane Hugo in 1989 what happens when a company's "lifelines" (phone, power, water, sewer, gas, transportation) are compromised. With the loss of electricity because of the hurricane, an electrolytic mixture in the manufacture of aluminum solidified prematurely in 350 vats at the plant. This and other storm-related damages amounted to $30 million.[17]

According to Pacific Bell, "It's usually not downed phone lines that strain the phone system during a disaster; it's network overload. This happens when a sudden flood of calls comes in or goes out of the disaster area . . . This is not just an inconvenience. Emergency workers rely on the phone system during a disaster."[18]

When a gas main explosion in a metropolitan center severed communications lines, many businesses found themselves cut off from their regular telecommunications channels. However, a major insurance company continued to do business, using a special service of the phone company. The phone company was also able to help a firm involved in a major product recall when it was deluged with incoming calls that threatened to jam the company's primary trunk lines.[19]

PUBLIC RELATIONS WORKSHEET

Assigned to: ______________________ Date Due: ______________

During and following a disaster, it's critical that your company communicate with the outside world to get help, and maintain contact with customers, suppliers, and employees.

- ✔ How will the public be kept informed of the situation, if that is appropriate?
- ✔ How will employees be notified of the status of recovery and whether to report to work?
- ✔ How will customers be notified?
- ✔ Who will be the spokesperson for the organization?
- ✔ What is the chain of command for determining the disaster notification messages and information that will be distributed?
- ✔ Should the disaster occur during off-hours, does the company need to have an automatic emergency notification system to summon key employees to preassigned locations?
- ✔ Can your local phone company help identify alternate systems for maintaining contact with the public?
- ✔ Is a cell phone available for communication? Does the cell phone service provider have an automatic cut-off/shutdown rule for higher-than-normal call levels? Do you know how to deactivate that system?

Comments: ____

____

____

____

____

____

PART V

Step Three: Recovery and Restoration

ENACTING EMERGENCY FUNCTIONS

> *"We've got a plan in place. Our fire fighters would do damage assessments in their districts and report back to us. But in reality, we don't have the resources to do everything. Our priorities would be large gathering places—schools, hospitals, apartment blocks. Single-family dwellings would go right to the bottom of the list. Our policy would pretty much be, 'Let it burn.'"*
>
> —Salt Lake City Assistant Fire Chief Robert Swenson.[20]

Following a disaster, it is most critical to immediately perform activities that protect the safety and welfare of employees and secure the building. In a community-wide disaster, experts believe that in some cases it will be impossible for police and fire departments to respond to calls for assistance. Therefore, businesses must plan for how they will respond to life- and property-threatening situations.

Here are some of the questions that should be addressed in planning for that response.

First Aid

How will you ensure that the most seriously injured are treated first?

____

____

Where will the first-aid supplies be stored? How will they be distributed during a disaster?

____

____

Do you have sufficient staff in appropriate locations to perform first aid if police and fire services are unavailable for 72 hours?

____

____

ENACTING EMERGENCY FUNCTIONS (continued)

Do you know the locations of designated sites in your community for first aid after a disaster?

Housing

Will the company be able to shelter employees in place if they are unable to leave your facility?

Do you have adequate food and other supplies for at least 72 hours?

Do you know the locations of designated mass-shelter sites in the community?

Transportation

Does each of the company's locations have access to a four-wheel drive vehicle should roadways be impassable?

What kind of a system should be established for carpooling for essential staff if they are unable to use their own vehicles or public transportation?

What kind of a system do you need for ensuring that vehicles always have, at a minimum, 1/3 of a tank of gas?

____

____

Rescue

Does the company have the equipment needed to conduct light search-and-rescue activities in your building(s) if police and fire services are unavailable?

____

____

Where will you store the rescue equipment so that it is accessible immediately following a disaster?

____

____

Who on staff is or can be trained to be a member of a search-and-rescue team?

____

____

What mechanism is established to account for the whereabouts of all employees and visitors immediately following a disaster?

____

____

ENACTING EMERGENCY FUNCTIONS (continued)

Evacuation

What criteria will be used to determine whether evacuation is necessary? Who will make the decision to evacuate? What if that person is unavailable?

Do you have a list of the materials, equipment, and supplies that will be most essential to continuing operations at an alternate location?

How will staff be notified of evacuation? Is an evacuation plan posted?

Is there a system for tracking who has been evacuated and who still remains in the building?

Is a nearby location designated to which staff can be evacuated in case the roads are impassable?

Is the evacuation plan flexible enough to cover all of the disasters identified as probable in Part I?

Assessment

Does the company have a checklist for summarizing the condition of the staff and visitors, the status of the building, and the need for medical assistance, fire services, search-and-rescue and other resources? (See page 67.)

____

____

Has a system been designated for taking physical inventory to determine casualties, the need to turn off the power, and the need to evacuate personnel?

____

____

Does the company have a system for identifying hazardous material spills resulting from the disaster?

____

____

ENACTING EMERGENCY FUNCTIONS (continued)

Security

What method will be used to secure the building if windows are broken or doors no longer lock?

How will looting be prevented if the building must be evacuated?

Have you contacted an outside security service to establish the company's needs immediately following a disaster?

If you have an automated security system, do you know how long the system can function without power? Is it tested regularly? Do you know what provisions the vendor has made for alternate arrangements?

LEARNING FROM EXPERIENCE

Turning off the gas after a disaster sounds like the right thing to do, but it isn't always appropriate. After the Loma Prieta earthquake, 155,000 residential customers turned off their gas; 145,000 of the shut-offs proved to be unnecessary. Turning the gas back on required gas company employees. It was five weeks before service was fully restored.[21]

SHARING INFORMATION

As your company's Disaster Response Teams assigned to various locations check in to provide information and request assistance, having a standardized system for sharing information is helpful. Here is a sample of the kind of simple reporting form you can provide for each Disaster Response Team or site manager.

Disaster Site Information Report

Location ______________________ Reporter ______________________

Day ______________________ Time ______________________

Number of individuals on site ____ Number of nonemployees ____

Number of children ____ Number with special needs ____

Key personnel present:

Number Injured:

____ Life-threatening injury ____ Require hospitalization

____ Need field first aid ____ Need search-and-rescue

Number Dead: ____

Damage to Property:

Damage threatening life or injury ______________________
Damage causing potential additional problems ______________________
Status of computer system ______________________
Status of records ______________________
Nonfunctioning: ❑ Phone ❑ Power ❑ Water ❑ Sewer
Other damage causing delay in operations restoration ______________________

Resources Needed:

❑ Rescue equipment ❑ Food/Water ❑ Blankets

Comments:

EMERGENCY COMMAND CENTER

To coordinate the flow of information, assignment of staff, and requests for resources and equipment, it is recommended that an Emergency Communications Center (ECC) be established following a disaster. This Center can be something as obvious as the company president's office or the employee break room. It should meet a few simple criteria:

- The ECC must be free of hazards that would be likely to compromise it following a disaster. A room with a lot of windows, for example, might be ideal if the most likely disaster is a power outage and natural light would be needed. The same room would be inappropriate, however, if an earthquake is likely to shatter those windows.

- The ECC should be equipped with a battery-operated radio, television, cell phone, and other supplies and equipment needed to maintain contact with outside and internal locations.

- Everyone in the company should know which room has been selected, so they know where to go to exchange information.

- If the company has a phone system that is tied to the power supply, the ECC should be equipped with a dedicated, hard-wired phone line.

- It's important to designate an alternate command center, too, that is away from your facility, in case the primary site is inaccessible.

- The ECC should have copies of your disaster plan and an updated list of employees and their phone numbers and emergency contacts.

- In a large operation, it may be helpful to provide emergency workers with color-coded tags indicating their assigned activity or special skills. Keep these in the ECC.

- Consider how long you expect the disaster to last. Assign the most experienced and skilled staff to work staggered shifts at the ECC, so there is fresh assistance available at all times.

GIVING LIFE TO YOUR PLAN

Once you've completed the process of preparing a disaster plan, don't put it on a shelf and let it gather dust! Here is what you should do to guarantee that you and your employees will be ready when a disaster strikes:

- ***Distribute the plan to every employee.*** During and after a disaster, employees may be called upon to perform functions they are normally not assigned to do. It is important that they are familiar with all aspects of the plan, so that it is indeed the practical guide they can use to step in and perform critical functions.

- ***Keep the plan within reach.*** Be sure employees, senior staff, and especially members of the Disaster Response Team have copies of the plan in their cars and homes. That way, if disaster strikes and the company facilities are inaccessible, the plan can still be implemented.

- ***Test the plan.*** A full-scale drill may be impossible, but individual departments can conduct "mock" drills so that each employee knows what should be done. You may prefer to test portions of the plan, such as search-and-rescue, evacuation, security, and first aid. And be sure to test the plan more frequently if your company experiences high employee turnover.

- ***Periodically train groups of new employees*** so that they know about the plan.

- ***Review the plan and your disaster supplies annually.*** This ensures that the information still makes sense, that all supplies are on hand, and that every employee is up-to-date on the plan contents and knows his or her role.

- ***Provide employees with summaries of what specifically is expected of them.*** Customize these summaries to each employee. This one-page summary should include phone numbers of who they should call, locations of where to report, and assignments to specific function Task Groups. Make this document a part of each employee's annual performance evaluation.

This is an important step, so mark your calendar to be sure you plan ahead. You don't want all of your hard work in preparing this plan to be wasted as it gathers dust on a shelf somewhere!

HOW TO MAINTAIN INTEREST

No matter how committed senior management is to the development of a disaster plan, and despite consistent effort to stay prepared, initial enthusiasm is bound to drop off as other projects surface and other priorities demand the company's attention. Here are some tips for maintaining interest:

- ✔ Take advantage of national and local events that focus on disaster preparedness. For example, April is Disaster Preparedness Month, September is National Fire Safety Month, one week in October is designated National Fire Prevention Week. Use these events as triggers for the annual review of your disaster plan; for renewing the company's disaster supplies; for checking your radio batteries and smoke detectors.

- ✔ Give new employees copies of the readiness pamphlets available from FEMA and the Red Cross, and be sure everyone understands the company's commitment to disaster planning.

- ✔ Make disaster drills fun by combining them with an event such as a company picnic.

- ✔ Issue a newsletter quarterly (see following sample) with tips and suggestions for staying prepared, and with news of progress being made on the company's readiness. Include recognition to employees who have contributed to moving forward with the plan. Keep the newsletter brief so that it doesn't become a big production that could delay its publication.

  Even if you issue a newsletter like this only once a year and use mostly material obtained from the Red Cross and other sources, just reminding employees about the importance of disaster planning is a very important part of maintaining everyone's interest.

SAMPLE NEWSLETTER

BE PREPARED

The Disaster Preparedness Newsletter
for the Box Paper Company
Jones, California

Volume I Number 1 Spring Issue

Payroll Unit First to Complete Disaster Plan Questions

Working with co-chairs Jane Gordon and Alex Gonzalez, the payroll unit last week completed its first draft of a written disaster plan to ensure that all Box Paper employees continue to receive pay immediately following a disaster.

Jane, Alex, and their subcommittee of Paul Smith and Jack Jones met with First Commercial Bank reps to determine what system would be used and what records would need to be maintained.

"We're quite confident that the plan we have created will stand up to any disaster we could experience. We know that will be a relief to all of us," Jane said.

Fire Department Visits Box Paper

At the invitation of the Disaster Preparedness Committee, Jones Fire Department Captain Paul Adams is scheduled to visit next week. He will help the Disaster Preparedness Committee identify hazards that could result in damage or injuries following a disaster. Check your Hazard Mitigation checklist to see if you are prepared for the visit. This meeting will convene in the cafeteria at 3:30 P.M. Friday.

Disaster Supplies Ordered and in Place Throughout Jones Facility

Thanks to Steve Exposito and the shipping and maintenance crews, all emergency supplies needed for Box Paper immediately following a disaster have been received. These supplies are now stored in six locations throughout the company.

The supplies include flashlights, battery-operated radios, first-aid items, food and water, and search-and-rescue equipment.

"I sincerely hope we never need to use even one item in our arsenal," said Box Paper President Pete Goodings. "But I know everyone is relieved that the supplies are here and we are ready."

Disaster Drill Scheduled for August

Disaster Preparedness Coordinator Ginger Jones has scheduled Box Paper's first ever "drill" to test draft plans. The walkthrough will take place on May 15, from 9:30 to 11:30 A.M., in the cafeteria. Although only managers will participate in this "table-top" event, Ginger is encouraging all interested employees to attend and observe.

Get your home disaster checklist flyer by calling Ginger at 52188.

PART VI

Your Business and the Community

LENDING YOUR HELP WHEN OTHERS ARE STRICKEN

During some disasters, only portions of each community are affected. If your company is lucky enough to be spared the impact of a disaster, you should consider how you can help other people and businesses that aren't so fortunate. Here are some suggestions:

- During your disaster planning stage, determine where your staff can report if volunteers are needed. Set up a company policy for providing paid leave for staff who volunteer.

- Consider in advance whether your company has supplies or equipment that could be donated or loaned in a community-wide disaster effort. Identify individuals and organizations in the community who should be contacted to provide donations.

- Participate in community-wide disaster drills so that your business is ready to play its own role in restoring the city or town where your business is located.

HOME DISASTER PREPAREDNESS

Up to four feet of muddy water oozed into Patricia and Robert Walker's three-bedroom home in northern Kentucky after torrential rains send the nearby Licking River flooding through their rural town. The floors of their one-story frame house are warped. Almost everything inside is ruined . . . Outside, their waterlogged 1989 Plymouth Acclaim is history. Yet the Walkers consider themselves lucky . . . they have flood insurance to cover their home repairs . . . Thousands of others whose lives were disrupted by winter floods or tornadoes also face a lengthy rebuiliding process that will continue . . . How well they recover will depend partly on how well they've prepared for the financial fallout of a natural disaster. That means carrying adequate insurance coverage, maintaining a household inventory, keeping important documents in a safe spot, and having an evacuation plan.[22]

As any business moves into the response and then the recovery stages following a disaster, employees' commitment and dedication are needed to minimize disruption and restore operations as quickly as possible. Employees who have not conducted disaster planning for their families are likely to be so preoccupied with the status of their homes and family members that they will be unavailable to assist in the task of recovery.

The American Red Cross and FEMA have excellent brochures available to aid in home disaster readiness: use them. To encourage employees in their individual preparations, distribute these pamphlets and other written material to new employees when they are hired, as part of the human resources and orientation process.

Here are some tips for home disaster preparedness. You may want to rewrite these and include them in what you provide for your employees:

- **HAVE A PLAN.** Encourage every employee to develop a plan with his/her family. The plan should describe where family members will meet if their home is uninhabitable, and should include designation of a friend in another community who can be called by family members to check in if the local phone system is compromised. Family members should know which areas of the house are safest in particular disasters and the emergency routes to use to evacuate the home. Evacuation plans should include a priority list of what should be taken, if there is time. Such items as medication, family photos, computer disks, and other nonreplaceable items should be listed first. The evacuation list should be posted in a central location in the home.

- **EMERGENCY SUPPLIES.** Employees should ensure that their homes are equipped with adequate food, water, and first aid and shelter supplies to last at least 72 hours. Provisions should be made for family pets. In addition, private vehicles should be equipped with essential medication, flashlights, blankets, emergency food and water, first-aid kits, warm and comfortable clothes, and sturdy shoes. At their desks, employees should also have access to sufficient food and water, a flashlight, portable radio, gloves and sturdy shoes.

- **VEHICLES.** Because power failures will make most gas pumps inoperable, gas tanks in private (and company-owned) vehicles should never be allowed to be less than 1/3 full. This is especially important if evacuation is necessary. An extra set of car keys should be stored with emergency supplies.

CASH. Power failures may mean that automatic teller machines will not be accessible and that banks will be closed. Keep some cash in bills of small denominations with the emergency supplies, for buying food and additional supplies during an emergency.

- **FAMILY DOCUMENTS.** Important papers should be stored in a waterproof container. Extra copies of insurance policies and other information should be stored away from home. (The company may want to consider providing small, on-site safety deposit boxes in which employees can keep their important personal documents and emergency cash.)

COMMUNICATIONS. Know which radio stations in the community will broadcast emergency information. Have a battery-powered radio. Be sure all family members have memorized the phone number of a relative or friend in another community who can act as the message center. Teach children to use 911 appropriately. Post emergency phone numbers in accessible and visible locations.

RESOURCES. Local phone books often contain valuable information about how to prepare for and what to do during disasters.

"It doesn't require any big process. It's just a matter of taking some time and saying 'Here's what I need.' A lot of people are surprised by disaster simply because they never thought about it."

—Rocky Lopes, American Red Cross[23]

HOME DISASTER PREPAREDNESS (continued)

Home Preparedness Checklist

- ❑ Make a plan for responding to a disaster, including escape routes.
- ❑ Practice the plan.
- ❑ Get emergency supplies.
- ❑ Check for and correct hazards.
- ❑ Take inventory of your personal property, and videotape or photograph it for insurance purposes.
- ❑ Install smoke detectors and fire extinguishers.
- ❑ Take a first aid/CPR class.
- ❑ Teach all adults and responsible teens how to shut off gas, water, and electricity—and *when* to do it.
- ❑ Teach all adults and responsible teens how to use fire extinguishers.

Comments: ______________________________

____

____

____

____

____

You've done it! If you've made it to the end of this book and completed even some of the lists and plans we've suggested, you should be feeling pretty comfortable about how your company will do if a disaster strikes. Good luck—and don't forget that disaster planning has to be an *ongoing* effort. Practice your plan, revise it, share it with new employees, and be aware of conditions in your community so you can be ready when disaster strikes.

"Too many planners put together an effective plan and then think they can rest on their laurels—constant effort is required to assimilate new lessons and incorporate them into the planning . . . Never assume you know too much! No matter how good your plan and planning group [are], there are new lessons to be learned from each disaster that occurs—take advantage of others' experience to learn lessons for use by your organizations."[24]

OTHER DISASTER PLANNING RESOURCES

- *Emergency Management Guide for Business and Industry*
  Emergency Preparedness Checklist
  Are You Ready
  (and many other publications)

  Federal Emergency Management Agency
  P.O. Box 70274
  Washington, DC 20024
  http://www.fema.gov
  1-800-480-2530

  American Red Cross
  http://www.redcross.org

  Or consult your phone book for your local chapter

- *Are You Ready for a Disaster—A Corporate Guide for Preparedness and Response*

  Manufacturers Alliance for Productivity and Innovation
  1525 Wilson Blvd., Suite 900
  Arlington, VA 22209
  703-841-9000

- *Earthquake Preparedness Training for Businesses*
  Business Resumption Planning Guidelines

  California Office of Emergency Services
  101 8th St., Suite 152
  Oakland, CA 94607

- *Business Contingency Planning*

  Disaster Recovery Solutions
  Pacific Bell
  1-800-953-1211

ENDNOTES

1. Northern California Disaster Network. Network news, vol. 1, no. 1, September 1992.

2. California Office of Emergency Services. Business Resumption Planning Guidelines (June 1993): vii.

3. Bay Area Regional Earthquake Preparedness Project (BAYREPP). Earthquake Preparedness Training for Businesses (June 1990): p. 1–4.

4. California Office of Emergency Services. Business Resumption Planning Guidelines (June 1993): 40.

5. BAYREPP. "Taking Care of Business," vol. 4, no. 2 (Summer 1989): p. 3–5.

6. BAYREPP. Earthquake Preparedness Training for Business (June 1990): p. 4–2. Quoting Earthquake Engineering Research Institute.

7. Sharon Cohen, Associated Press. "Grand Forks: Flood gone but devastation remains," San Francisco Examiner, July 6, 1997, sec. A-10.

8. BAYREPP. Earthquake Preparedness Training for Business (June 1990): p. 6–1.

9. Ibid., p. 5–1. Quoting Biopharm, "Shock Waves at Cetus."

10. Federal Emergency Management Agency (FEMA). Emergency Management Guide for Business and Industry (1993): p. 44.

11. Sharon Cohen, Associated Press. "Grand Forks: Flood gone but devastation remains," San Francisco Examiner, July 6, 1997, sec. A-10.

12. BAYREPP. "Taking Care of Business," vol. 4, no. 2 (Summer 1989): p. 4.

13. Manufacturers Alliance for Productivity and Innovation (MAPI). "Are You Ready for Disaster?" (April 1990). Quoting the Flint Journal, October 10, 1989.

14. BAYREPP. "Taking Care of Business," vol. 4, no. 2 (Summer 1989): p. 14.

15. MAPI. "Are You Ready for Disaster?" (April 1990): p. 47.

ENDNOTES (continued)

16. BAYREPP. Earthquake Preparedness Training for Business (June 1990): p. 7–1.

17. MAPI. "Are You Ready for Disaster?" (April 1990): p. 47. Quoting The Washington Post, November 19, 1989.

18. Pacific Bell. Calling (April 1997).

19. Pacific Bell Business Contingency Planning. Disaster Recovery Solutions Guide, p. 22–23.

20. " 'Big One's Big Threat in Utah," San Francisco Examiner, April 6, 1997, sec. C-13.

21. "On Solid Ground," San Francisco Chronicle, January 19, 1994, p. 6.

22. Associated Press. "When Natural Disaster Strikes," March 26, 1997.

23. Ibid.

24. California Office of Emergency Services. Business Resumption Planning Guidelines (June 1993): p. 40.

NOTES

NOTES

TITLES IN THE VIVA-CRISP 50 MINUTE SERIES

ISBN	Title / Author Price Rs. 99/- Each
	ADULT LEARNING
— 8176495131	**Basic Business Math** by Richard P. Truchon
— 8176495697	**Formatting Letters and Reports** by Eleanor Davidson
— 8176496901	**Improve Your Reading Improve Your Job** by Jeanne Miller
— 817649710X	**Study Skills Strategies** by Uelaine Lengefeld
— 8176497118	**Successful Life Long Learning** by Robert Steinbach
— 8176497320	**Vocabulary Improvement** by Diana Bonet
	CALL CENTER SUCCESS
— 8176495271	**Call Center Success** by Lloyd C. Finch
	CHANGE
— 8176495387	**Coping With Workplace Change** by J. Jeffreys
— 8176495875	**Managing Change at Work** by C. Scott & D. Jaffe
— 8176495913	**Managing Personal Change** by C. Scott & Dennis Jaffe
— 8176497282	**Understanding Organizational Change** by L. Fossum
	COACHING AND MENTORING
— 8176495166	**Be Your Own Coach** by B. Braham & C. Wahl
— 817649531X	**Coaching and Counseling** by Marianne Minor
— 8176495328	**Coaching for Development** by Marianne Minor
— 8176495859	**Making the Most of Being Mentored** by Gordon F. Shea
— 8176495999	**Mentoring** by Gordon F. Shea
	COMPLIANCE
— 8176495522	**Disaster Preparedness** by J. Freestone & R. Raab
	CONFLICT RESOLUTION
— 8176495883	**Managing Disagreement Constructively** by Herbert S. Kindler
	CREATIVITY
— 8176495417	**Creative Decision Making** by H. B. Gelatt
— 8176495425	**Creativity in Business** by Carol Kinsey Goman
	CUSTOMER SERVICE
— 8176496839	**A Positive Guide to Superior Service** by William Martin
— 8176495018	**Beyond Customer Service** by Richard F. Gerson
— 8176496863	**Calming Upset Customers** by Rebecca Morgan
— 8176495441	**Customer Satisfaction** by Dru Scott
— 8176495921	**Managing Quality Customer Service** by William B. Martin

	ISBN	Title / Author	Price Rs. 99/- Each
—	8176495972	**Measuring Customer Satisfaction** by R. Gerson	
—	817649691X	**Most Customer Services Start With the Telephone** by Nancy Friedman	
		ELECTRONIC COMMUNICATION	
—	817649738X	**Writing Effective E-Mail** by Nancy Flynn	
		FINANCE	
—	8176495050	**The Accounting Cycle** by J. Jacquet & W. Miller	
—	8176495855	**Basics of Budgeting** by Terry Dickey	
—	8176495689	**Financial Analysis** by J. Gill & M. Chatton	
—	8176496987	**Personal Financial Fitness** by Allen Klosowski	
—	817649707X	**Starting Your New Business** by Charles Martin	
—	8176497290	**Understanding Financial Statements** by James Gill	
		HIRING AND MANAGING	
—	817649500X	**50 One-Minute Tips for Recruiting Employees** by Hayes & Ninemeier	
—	8176494526	**50 One-Minute Tips for Retaining Employees** by Hayes & Nlnemeier	
—	8176495034	**About Pay** by James F. Carey	
—	8176495115	**Attacking Absenteeism** by Lynn Tylczak	
—	8176495174	**Behavior-Based Interviewing** by Terry Fitzwater	
—	817649559X	**Effective Recruiting Strategies** by R. Visconti & M. Brounstein	
—	817649562X	**Employee Suggestion Systems** by C. Martin & R. Bassford	
—	8176495751	**High Performance Hiring** by Robert Wendover	
—	8176496995	**Personnel Testing** by John Jones	
—	8176497037	**Quality Interviewing** by Robert Maddux	
—	8176497045	**Recruiting for High Performance** by Robert Wendover	
—	8176497363	**Writing a Human Resources Manual** by S. Brock & S. Cabbell	
		INCREASE EMPLOYEE PERFORMANCE	
—	8176495530	**Downsizing Without Disaster** by Lynn Tylczak	
—	8176495573	**Effective Performance Appraisals** by Robert B. Maddux	
—	8176495638	**Empowerment** by C. Scott & D. Jaffe	
—	8176495743	**Handling the Difficult Employee** by Marty Brounstein	
—	8176495867	**Managing Anger** by Rebecca Luhn Wolfe	
—	8176495891	**Managing for Commitment** by Carol Kinsey Goman	
—	8176495905	**Managing Negative People** by S. Michael Kravitz	
—	8176496960	**Partners in Performance** by Tony Moglia	

ISBN	Title / Author	Price Rs. 99/- Each
JOBS AND CAREERS		
— 817649528X	**Career Discovery Program** by Elwood N. Chapman	
— 8176495409	**Creating Your Skills Portfolio** by Carrie Straub	
— 8176495565	**Effective Networking** by Venda Raye-Johnson	
— 8176495719	**Getting Hired** by Richard Pinsker	
— 8176494569	**Networking for Success** by Nancy Flynn	
— 8176496944	**Preparing for the Behavior-Based Interview** by T. Fitzwater	
— 8176497002	**Preparing for Your Interview** by Diane Berk	
— 8176497088	**Strategic Resumes** by Marci Mahoney	
— 817649741X	**Your First Thirty Days** by E. Chapman & R. Maddux	
MANAGEMENT SKILLS		
— 8176495468	**Delegating For Results** by Robert B. Maddux	
— 8176495735	**Goals and Goal Setting** by Larrie A. Rouillard	
— 8176495778	**Improving Your Company Image** by Sylvia Blishak	
— 8176495948	**Managing the Technical Professional** by Herbert Kindler	
— 8176494550	**Multipoint Feedback** by D. Jude-York & S. Wise	
— 8176494577	**Project Management** by Marion E. Haynes	
— 8176497053	**Retaining Your Employees** by B. Wingfield & J. Berry	
— 8176497126	**Successful Negotiation** by Robert B. Maddux	
— 8176497215	**The Ecstatic Buzz of Doing Business** by J. Bado & C. Ivanacic	
— 8176495808	**The Internal Consultant** by Marcia Meislin	
MANUFACTURING AND INVENTORY		
— 817649514X	**Basics of Inventory Management** by J. Viale	
— 8176495158	**Basics of Manufacturing** by J. Viale	
— 8176495182	**Benchmarking Basics** by James Patterson	
— 8176495212	**Building a Total Quality Culture** by Joe Batten	
— 8176495816	**JIT Forecasting and Master Scheduling** by J. Viale	
— 8176495379	**The Continuously Improving Self** by J. Lickson	
— 8176497258	**TQM** by JoAnn Haberer & M. Webb	
PEER RELATIONS & APPEARANCE		
— 8176495247	**Business Etiquette & Professionalism** by M. Kay duPont	
— 817649576X	**Improving Peer Relationships** by Norman Hill	
— 8176495786	**Influence** by Elaina Zuker	
— 8176495794	**Influencing Others** by William Nothstine	
— 8176495956	**Managing Upward** by Patti Hathaway	

ISBN	Title / Author	Price Rs. 99/- Each
— 8176496936	**Office Politics** by Rebecca Luhn Wolfe	
— 8176496979	**Personal Counseling** by R. Knowdell & E. Chapman	
— 8176494593	**Winning at Human Relations** by Elwood N. Chapman	
	PRESENTATION SKILLS	
— 8176495581	**Effective Presentation Skills** by Steve Mandel	
— 8176497185	**Technical Presentation Skills** by Steve Mandel	
— 8176497304	**Using Visual Aids** by C. Raines & L. Williamson	
	PRODUCTIVITY	
— 8176495085	**Achieving Results** by Lorna Riley	
— 8176495093	**Administrative Assistant** by Brenda Bailey-Hughes	
— 8176496820	**Plan Your Work: Work Your Plan** by James Sherman	
— 8176497134	**Successful Self-Management** by Paul R. Timm	
	SALES AND MARKETING	
— 8176496847	**Achieve Large-Budget Marketing Without a Large Budget** by Richard Gerson	
— 8176495204	**Building and Closing the Sale** by V. Thornton	
— 8176495263	**Business Research** by P. Timm & R. Farr	
— 8176495360	**Consultative Sales Power** by Karen Mantyla	
— 817649545X	**Dealing Effectively With the Media** by John Wade	
— 8176495514	**Direct Marketing Techniques** by Lois Geller	
— 8176495603	**Effective Sales Management** by Tom Johnson	
— 8176495964	**Marketing Your Consulting or Professional Services** by D. Karlson	
— 8176497029	**Prospecting: The Key to Sales Success** by Virden Thornton	
— 8176496774	**Sales Training Basics** by Elwood Chapman	
— 8176497339	**Winning the Inner Game of Selling** by Richard Gerson	
	SELF IMPROVEMENT	
— 8176495077	**Achieving Job Satisfaction** by Editors of Crisp Publications, Inc	
— 8176495123	**Attitude** by E. Chapman & W. Mcknight	
— 8176495298	**Clear and Creative Thinking** by Herb Kindler	
— 8176495344	**Concentration** by Sam Horn	
— 8176495433	**Critical Thinking** by Daniel A. Feldman	
— 8176495492	**Developing Positive Assertiveness** by Sam R. Lloyd	
— 8176495506	**Developing Self-Esteem** by Connie Palladino	
— 8176495646	**Ethics in Business** by R. Maddux & D. Maddux	
— 817649688X	**Finding Your Purpose** by Barbara J. Braham	

ISBN	Title / Author	Price Rs. 99/- Each
— 8176495980	**Memory Skills in Business** by Madelyn Burley-Allen	
— 8176497061	**Risk Taking** by Herbert Kindler	

STRATEGIC DEVELOPMENT

— 8176496871	**Competency and the Learning Organization** by Donald Shandler
— 8176495395	**Creating a Learning Organization** by Barbara Braham
— 8176496758	**Organization Development** by Lenny Ralphs
— 8176496952	**Organizational Vision, Values and Mission** by Scott, Jaffe & Tobe
— 8176497142	**Successful Strategic Planning** by Stephen Haines
— 8176497169	**Systematic Succession Planning** by Rebecca Wolfe
— 8176494585	**Understanding Leadership Competencies** by Guggenheimer & Szulc

STRESS, WELL-BEING & RETIREMENT

— 817649593X	**Managing Stress for Mental Fitness** by M. Raber & G. Dyck
— 8176497096	**Stress that Stress That Motivates** by Dru Scott

SUPERVISORY SKILLS

— 8176495042	**Accountability** by Sam R. Lloyd
— 8176495239	**Building Trust** by Mary Shurtleff
— 8176495654	**Excellence in Supervision** by Rick Conlow
— 8176495700	**From Technical Specialist to Supervisor** by Donald Shandler
— 8176497150	**Supervising for Success** by Tony Moglia
— 8176497223	**The New Supervisor** by Elwood N. Chapman

TEAM BUILDING AND LEADERSHIP

— 8176495069	**Achieving Consensus** by Jon Scott & Eileen Flanigan
— 8176495662	**Facilitation Skills for Team Leaders** by C. Martin & D. Hackett
— 8176495824	**Leadership Skills for Women** by M. Manning & P. Haddock
— 8176495832	**Learning to Lead** by E. N. Chapman & P. Heim
— 8176494542	**Motivating at Work** by Twyla Dell
— 8176496782	**Team Building** by Robert B. Maddux
— 8176497177	**Team Problem Solving** by Sandy Pokras
— 8176497312	**Virtual Teaming** by D. Jude-York & L. Davis
— 8176497347	**Working in Teams** by Sandy Pokras

TELEPHONE SKILLS

— 8176497207	**Telephone Courtesy & Customer Service** by Lloyd C. Finch

TIME MANAGEMENT

— 817649674X	**Office Management** by M. Manning & P. Haddock
— 8176496766	**Personal Time Management** by Marion E. Haynes

	ISBN	Title / Author	Price Rs. 99/- Each
—	8176497010	**Professionalism in the Office** by Marilyn Manning	
—	8176497231	**The Telephone and Time Management** by Dru Scott	
		TRAINING	
—	8176495026	**50 One-Minute Tips for Trainers** by Carrie Van Daele	
—	8176495352	**Conducting a Needs Analysis** by Geri McArdle	
—	8176495476	**Delivering Effective Training Sessions** by Geri McArdle	
—	8176495484	**Developing Instructional Design** by Geri McArdle	
—	8176495549	**Dynamics of Diversity** by Odette Pollar	
—	8176496898	**Graphics for Presenters** by Lynn Kearny	
—	8176497266	**Training Managers to Train** by David Hayes	
—	8176497274	**Training Methods That Work** by Lois Hart	
—	8176497355	**Working Together** by George Simons	
		VERBAL COMMUNICATION	
—	8176496731	**50 One-Minute Tips to Better Communication** by P. E. Bozek	
—	8176495336	**Communicating With Employees** by Frank M. Corrado	
—	8176495557	**Effective Meeting Skills** by Marion E. Haynes	
—	8176495611	**Emotional Intelligence Works** by M. Kravitz & S. D. Schubert	
—	8176495727	**Giving and Receiving Feedback** by Patti Hathaway	
—	8176495840	**Making Humor Work** by Terry Paulson	
—	8176495107	**The Art of Communicating** by Bert Decker	
—	8176495255	**The Business of Listening** by Diana Bonet	
—	817649724X	**Thinking on Your Feet** by Marlene Caroselli	
		WRITTEN COMMUNICATION	
—	8176495190	**Better Business Writing** by Susan L. Brock	
—	8176495301	**Clear Writing** by Diana Bonet	
—	8176495670	**Fat-Free Writing** by Carol Andrus	
—	8176496928	**Powerful Proofreading Skills** by D. Smith & H. Sutton	
—	8176497193	**Technical Writing in the Corporate World** by H. Estrin & N. Elliot	
—	8176495220	**The Building Blocks of Business Writing** by Jack Swenson	
—	8176497371	**Writing Business Proposals and Reports** by Susan L. Brock	
—	8176497398	**Writing Fitness** by Jack Swenson	
—	8176497401	**Writing That Sells** by Kathleen A. Begley	

Prices are subject to change without notice.